Engaging Hymnody

Volume 1: Advent/Christmas

Alternative Introductions, Accompaniments, and Interpretations for Today's Congregational Song

by
Robert LeBlanc

LITURGICAL PRESS
Collegeville, Minnesota

www.litpress.org

ACKNOWLEDGMENTS

Cover design: Monica Bokinskie. Photo courtesy of Getty Images.

ISBN: 978-0-8146-4406-5

Contents

Foreword

Engaging Hymnody is a new collection of contemporary settings for organ of most of the best-known hymn tunes that Christians have sung at worship throughout the centuries. These melodies have borne the faith of the church with a variety of texts for many generations and have stood the test of time. While the tunes themselves have been frequently associated with a particular text in different denominations, more recent hymnals have employed these tunes in the service of new contemporary texts. Many composers have been producing new music for new texts. But there's another more practical technique at one's disposal—one less burdensome to a congregation struggling with too much new music. Analogous to the gospel itself, which is "ever ancient, ever new," these same tunes can live again in contemporary harmonic language that wakens singers to hear the gospel in a way that speaks to our own generation.

Music directors sometimes err in trying to teach too much new music too fast. Their congregations, who necessarily learn at a slower pace, are at times overwhelmed by being constantly challenged. This technique of repurposing melodies that are already in people's collective memory has proven itself throughout music history. It requires only our own creativity and dedication to our ministry to bring it alive for our contemporaries.

I offer these settings for your consideration and use in the hope that they may open the ears and hearts of congregations to the texts that both express and further form us through worship. I urge the greatest flexibility in their employment.

Robert LeBlanc

I. "Savior of the Nations, Come"

NUN KOMM, DER HEIDEN HEILAND

Robert LeBlanc

Tune: NUN KOMM, DER HEIDEN HEILAND, 77 77, *Geistliche Gesangbüchlein,* Wittenberg, 1524.

II. Chorale Partita on "People, Look East"

BESANÇON

Robert LeBlanc

Tune: BESANÇON CAROL, 87 89 87, French carol.

IV.
I.
II.
ped.
V.
II.
I.

VI.
ped.

III. "O Come, Divine Messiah"

VENEZ, DIVIN MESSIE Robert LeBlanc

Tune: VENEZ, DIVIN MESSIE, 7 8 7 6 with refrain; French Noël, 16th cent.
Music: *Engaging Hymnody,* © 2019, Robert LeBlanc, b. 1948. Published and administered by Liturgical Press, Collegeville, MN 56321.

II.
II.
I.

IV. "Lo, How a Rose E'er Blooming"

ES IST EIN ROS' ENTSPRUNGEN

Robert LeBlanc

I.

II.

Tune: ES IST EIN ROS' ENTSPRUNGEN, German, 16th cent.; *Speierischen Gesangbuch,* Cologne, 1599.

III.
ped.

V. "Of the Father's Love Begotten"

DIVINUM MYSTERIUM

Robert LeBlanc

Tune: DIVINUM MYSTERIUM, 87 87 87 7, Didrik Petersen of Abo.

III.
ped.

VI. Chorale Partita on "God Rest You Merry, Gentlemen"

GOD REST YOU MERRY Robert LeBlanc

Tune: GOD REST YOU MERRY, 76 76 86 with refrain; 18th cent. English carol.
Music: *Engaging Hymnody,*

II.
II.
I.
(man.)
(ped.)

III.
II.
I.
I.
II.

IV.
II.
I.
ped.
(man.)
(ped.)

VII. "Angels We Have Heard on High"

GLORIA

Robert LeBlanc

Tune: GLORIA, 77 77 with refrain, traditional French carol.

Music: *Engaging Hymnody,* © 2019, Robert LeBlanc, b. 1948. Published and administered by Liturgical Press, Collegeville, MN 56321.

VERSE 2
man.
to refrain
VERSE 3
II.
I.
ped.
to refrain
VERSE 4
man.
to refrain

VIII. "O Little Town of Bethlehem"

ST. LOUIS

Robert LeBlanc

Tune: ST. LOUIS, 86 86 86 86, Lewis H. Redner, 1831–1908.

III.

IX. "It Came upon a Midnight Clear"

CAROL

Robert LeBlanc

Tune: CAROL, 86 86 86 86, Richard S. Willis, 1819–1900.

II.
II.
I.
ped.

X. "Go Tell It on the Mountain"

GO TELL IT ON THE MOUNTAIN

Robert LeBlanc

Tune: GO TELL IT ON THE MOUNTAIN, 76 76 with refrain; African-American spiritual.

XI. "Silent Night"

STILLE NACHT

Robert LeBlanc

Tune: STILLE NACHT, Irregular, Franz Gruber, 1820–1885.

XII. "Joy to the World"

ANTIOCH

Robert LeBlanc

Tune: ANTIOCH, CM with repeat; arr. from George F. Handel, 1685–1759, in T. Hawkes' *Collection of Tunes,* 1833.
Music: *Engaging Hymnody,* © 2019, Robert LeBlanc, b. 1948. Published and administered by Liturgical Press, Collegeville, MN 56321.

II.
II.
I.
ped.
II.
ped.